HELLO!

CATBOY © BENJI NATE
DESIGNED BY RACHEL DUKES
PUBLISHED BY SILVER SPROCKET
SUMMER 2017. PRINTED IN CANADA.
THIRD PRINTING. EARLY 2019.
SILVER SPROCKET CATALOGUE # 78

ISBN: 978-1-945509-15-5

MY CAT Henry IS MY BEST FRIEND.
I SAW A SHOOTING STAR AND WISHED HE COULD HANG OUT WITH ME LIKE A PERSON.
I THINK I SHOULD'VE BEEN MORE CAREFUL WITH MY WORDING.
G'MORNIN'.
MORNING...

HI, OLIVE !!
YOU KNOW MY NAME ?
HENRY
DUH.
THIS IS WEIRD, RIGHT?
HEY!! UMMM...
YOU'RE NOT WEARING ANY CLOTHES !
CAN I BORROW SOME ?
OKAY, BUT I ONLY HAVE LADY CLOTHES.
I DON'T KNOW WHAT THAT MEANS.
WELL, OK.

DO I LOOK OKAY?
YOU LOOK LOVELY!!
LOVELY!!
YOU HUNGRY?
I AM.
LET'S GET BREAKFAST BURRITOS.
I DON'T KNOW WHAT THAT MEANS.
BUT OKAY
COOL BOY

FOO
TRU
CAN WE GET...
... TWO BREAKFAST BURRITOS ?
YOU GOT IT.
COOL BOY
COOL BOY

BLEGH!

OH NO!
I'M STILL HUNGRY.

OH NO...
COOL BOY
SQUAWK!!

Y'KNOW...
YOU'RE WEIRDER THAN I THOUGHT YOU'D BE...
REALLY?
YEAH.

OH! I SAVED YOU SOME BIRD.
I THINK YOUR DIET IS LACKING BIRD.

SEE?
YOU'RE SUCH A CAT!!!

BUT I THINK WE CAN STILL BE PALS.
GOOD. ME TOO.
COOL BOY
COOL BOY

COOL

SO I WAS THINKING...
...WE SHOULD GO OUT AND TALK TO PEOPLE.

PEOPLE?
LIKE FRIENDS?
COOL BOY

I DON'T HAVE ANY FRIENDS...
BUT I THOUGHT MAYBE WITH YOU AROUND I'D HAVE SOME CONFIDENCE.
AND WE CAN BOTH MAKE SOME FRIENDS.

DO WE NEED FRIENDS?

OH, I DON'T KNOW.
SAY, WHAT ARE YOU READING?

I DUNNO.
I CAN'T READ...
HAHA

BAR
BEER
SO THIS IS A BAR...
YEP.

HA
HA
WOW
HA
HA
COOL BOY

IT'S SO LOUD!
YEAH

TWO BEERS PLEASE.
COOL BOY
CAN I GET MINE IN A BOWL?

EW!!
GROSS!!

AND THEN HE WAS LIKE...
HA HA HA HA HA HA HA
OMG
WHO IS SHE?
DIXIE?
WE WENT TO SCHOOL TOGETHER.
I HATE HER.
COOL BOY
SHE'S COOL!
NO SHE'S NOT!
WOW
HEY OLIVE.
I THOUGHT YOU MOVED, LIKE, FOUR YEARS AGO.
NOPE.
STILL HERE...
COOL
WHO'S YOUR PAL?
HI
MY PET CAT HENRY.
COOL

HENRY...
I LIKE THE WAY YOU DRESS.
THANK YOU...
IT'S MY CLOTHES.

I HAVE SOME FRIENDS YOU SHOULD MEET.
OK

COOL BOY.

WE'RE GOING!
WHERE?
HOME.

OK! WANNA ORDER A PIZZA?
YES.

I HAVE TO PEE SO BAD!
JUST GO IN THOSE BUSHES.!
HENRY

IS THAT OKAY?
BOYS DO IT ALL THE TIME!

OKAY...

THIS ISN'T WORKING.
I'M PEEING ALL OVER MY FEET.
I THINK YOU HAVE TO STAND UP.

ARE YOU SURE!?
I THINK!
AH! IT WORKS!
HENRY

YOU DON'T HAVE TO KICK IT!
ARE YOU SURE!?
KICK
KICK

HEY, HENRY?
DO YOU KNOW WHAT YOU WANT ON YOUR PIZZA?
ANCHOVIES!
GROSS!
ANCHOVIES ARE GOOD!
SHUT UP!
HM...
WHAT SHOULD WE WATCH?
OH! I KNOW!
WOW!
MROW
CAT PARTY
I GET TO PICK NEXT TIME...

HEY, OLIVE?
YEAH?

WAS I THIS CUTE WHEN I WAS A NORMAL CAT?

HMM...

MROW!
PURRR

NOT THAT CUTE, NO...

KNOCK KNOCK!
BUT...
WHAT ABOUT WHEN ...
PIZZA!

LOOK, PIZZA!!
NOTHING ELSE MATTERS NOW!

MUNCH
MUNCH
WANNA TRY IT?
OK...
I LIKE IT!

WHEN DID YOU GET A PHONE?
IT'S YOUR PHONE.
BUT DIXIE INVITED US TO HER HOUSEWARMING PARTY NEXT WEEK!
YOU GAVE HER MY NUMBER?
SHE THINKS IT'S MINE.
DO YOU WANNA GO?
OH, I DUNNO.
I'D HAVE TO GET AN OUTFIT,
THERE'S FREE FOOD.
I'LL THINK ABOUT IT...

YAWN!

YOU SLEEPY?
VERY.
ME TOO.

I DON'T THINK WE CAN SLEEP LIKE THIS ANYMORE.

IS THIS BETTER?
MUCH.

GOOD MORNING.
NO! THIS SUCKS!

HISSS!
Cool Boy
patch

WOW!
WHAT A NICE HOUSE!
IT'S TOO BIG!
DING DONG
HEY HENRY!
HI!
WE BROUGHT YOU SOME WINE.
I'M HERE TOO.
OH!!
THIS IS WHAT I USED TO DRINK WHEN I WAS A BROKE COLLEGE FRESHMAN IN LA!
IT'S PERFECT!
WOW...

WOW!
SO BIG AND BEAUTIFUL!
AW. THANK YOU HENRY!

I REFUSE TO GET MOST OF MY FURNITURE OUT OF STORAGE UNTIL MY DECORATOR COMES BY SO IT'S KIND OF SPARSE.

IT'S NOT BAD!
OUR LIVING ROOM IS JUST A PILE OF BLANKETS.
DON'T TELL HER THAT!
THAT'S SO COOL AND BOHEMIAN!
UGH.

THE CATERERS ARE SERVING CHAMPAGNE. PLEASE HELP YOURSELF.
THIS IS SO FANCY!
IS THIS HOW WE SHOULD LIVE?
NO.
SHOULD WE TRY TO MINGLE?
I GUESS.
ITS LIKE THEY'VE GOT A FORCE FIELD UP!
I CAN'T GET THROUGH!
HA HA HA HA HA HA HA HA
ABORT MISSION!

PSSST!
YOU WANNA GO EXPLORE?
CAN WE DO THAT?

ONLY IF IT'S SECRET!

THIS MUST BE THE DRAWING ROOM.

YOU DRAW SO WHY DON'T YOU HAVE ONE OF THESE?
THAT'S NOT WHAT THAT MEANS.

"DRAWING" IS SHORT FOR "WITHDRAWING."
OK, BUT LOOK!

SHE'S BEAUTIFUL.

YOU'RE THE PRETTIEST GIRL AT THIS PARTY.

AND MAYBE EVEN...

...THE WHOLE WORLD.
MIAOU!

SHE'S FRENCH!
BONJOUR!
I'M GONNA GO NOW.

AH!
OH!
I'M SORRY!

HI, I'M JEAN.
I'M OLIVE.
ARE YOU EXPLORING TOO?
YEP.

ITS NICE TO MEET A COOL 'N' CUTE GIRL WHO IS ALSO INTO TRESPASSING.
"CUTE"... "COOL"...?

HENRY!
WE GOTTA GO!!
WHAT!?
ALREADY?

THANKS FOR YOUR HELP, HENRY!
I'M NEVER BUSY!

THERE!

SO WHAT DO WE DO NOW?

NOW WE SIT HERE AND TRY TO SELL PAINTINGS!

OKAY!

THIS SUCKS!
WE'VE BEEN HERE FOR TWO HOURS!
I DON'T GET IT.
THE ONLY DIFFERENCE BETWEEN YOU AND THESE OTHER PEOPLE IS THAT THEY'RE GOOD AT ART.
BUT, LIKE, THATS THE ONLY DIFFERENCE.
I'M SEEING A BUNCHA FOLKS IN THE GALLERIES WITH GLASSES OF WINE.
WANT ME TO SNAG YOU SOME?
I DON'T THINK YOU CAN TAKE IT TO-GO.
WATCH ME.

THE WINE ZONE...
SO ARTSY!

BINGO!

DOUBLE BINGO!

WINE GUY
HE'S DISTRACTED!

SWIPE!
CLINK CLINK

HAHA!
LATER DAYS, FART FACES!
WINE + ART

LOOK!
I'M BACK!
YOU DID IT!!
CHEERS!!
NOW I TRULY FEEL LIKE AN ARTIST...
COOL BOY

...KINDA DRUNK, VERY SAD, AND KINDA HUNGRY.

WOW!
I MUST BE AN ARTIST TOO!
LET'S GET PIZZA!

I THINK WE SHOULD CALL IT A NIGHT AND PACK UP.
OKAY!

HEY! OLIVE, RIGHT?

HUH? WHAT?
OH, HI JEAN.

I'D LIKE TO BUY THAT PAINTING!
I DON'T HAVE CHANGE FOR THAT.
KEEP THE CHANGE!

WHAT WAS THAT!?
A SALE.

UGH!
THIS SUCKS!
WHAT'S WRONG?
I'M WORRIED I MIGHT NOT BE ABLE TO MAKE RENT THIS MONTH.
I THINK YOU HAVE TO GET A JOB.

I DON'T THINK A LIL OL' CAT LIKE MYSELF IS QUALIFIED TO WORK ANYWHERE.
WELL, WE HAVE TO TRY.

LET'S TAKE A WALK!

HELP WANTED
Cafe
LOOK!
THIS CAFE IS HIRING!
I'D GET FUR ALL UP IN PEOPLE'S COFFEES!

CAN I JUST DO SOMETHING COOL?
LIKE NAP FOR MONEY?

LET'S FIGURE OUT HOW TO MONETIZE NAPS...

HI HENRY.
AND HI OLIVE.
COOL BOY

WHAT ARE YOU DOING HERE, JEAN?

I WORK RIGHT AROUND THE CORNER.

AND WHO IS THIS?

THIS IS JENNY!

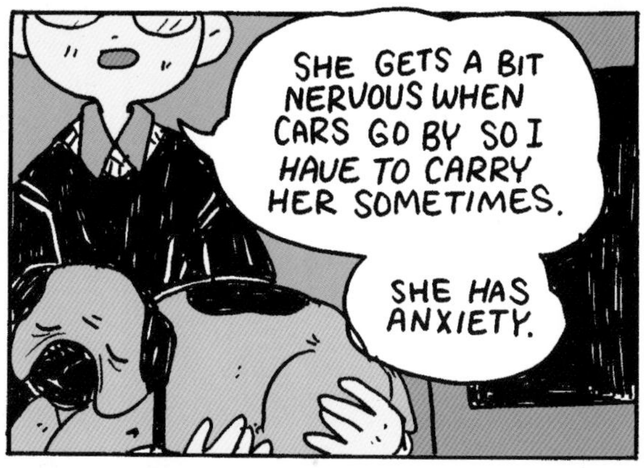
SHE GETS A BIT NERVOUS WHEN CARS GO BY SO I HAVE TO CARRY HER SOMETIMES.
SHE HAS ANXIETY.

WHAT TYPE OF CAT IS THAT?
SOME KIND OF EXOTIC SHORTHAIR?
IT'S A DOG.

WHATEVER IT IS I DON'T TRUST IT...

IT'S BEEN HARD TRYING TO FIND A PETSITTING PLACE THAT'LL SERVICE HER NEEDS...
GRRRR
GASP!

I HAVE AN IDEA!
HENRY'S LOOKIN' FOR A JOB...

...AND HE'S GOT ALL THE TIME IN THE WORLD...
GRRRR

I SEE WHERE YOU'RE GOING WITH THIS!
IT'S PERFECT!

HENRY! YOU'RE HIRED!
HUH?

GRRRR

OH YEAH!?
WELL, YOU'RE UGLY!

BE NICE!

SHE KNOWS SHE'S UGLY!

UGLY IN A CUTE WAY...

BOY

WHERE ARE YOU GOING?
WORK.
BOY
BOY
BUT WHAT ABOUT ME?
YOU GOTTA WORK TOO!
IT'S YOUR FIRST DAY PETSITTING ALONE.
I DON'T WANNA WORK!
NOBODY DOES...

I GUESS I'M ON MY OWN...
WHAT NOW?

MORNING LIST
1) BRUSH TEETH.
2) TAKE SHOWER.
3) PUT ON CLOTHES.
4) EAT BREAKFAST.
GOOD LUCK!
LOVE, Olive
OH.

1.) BRUSH TEETH.

2.) TAKE SHOWER.
LICK
LICK

3.) PUT ON CLOTHES.

4.) EAT BREAKFAST.
Henry

I DID IT!
COOL BOY

ZZZZ
INCOMING CALL: JEAN
ZZZZ

HELLO?

HI HENRY. IT'S JEAN.
I'M BRINGING JENNY OVER BUT I WAS WONDERING...
WONDERING WHAT?

WELL, I HAVE SOME PALS WHO NEED A PETSITTER TODAY...
SO I WAS WONDERING IF YOU WERE UP FOR THE JOB...
FOR MORE PIZZA MONEY?
YES!

KNOCK
KNOCK

THANKS HENRY!

OKAY YOU LITTLE FREAKS.
GET YOUR FOOD.

YOU'RE SCAREDY CATS.

BUT YOU'RE NOT SCARED.
JUST MEAN.
JENNY♡

WALK TIME!

WHINE!
SHUT UP.

STOP TRYING TO RUN AWAY!
I'M YOUR MASTER NOW!
STOP!
OH NO...
WE'RE DONE!
BACK TO THE APARTMENT!

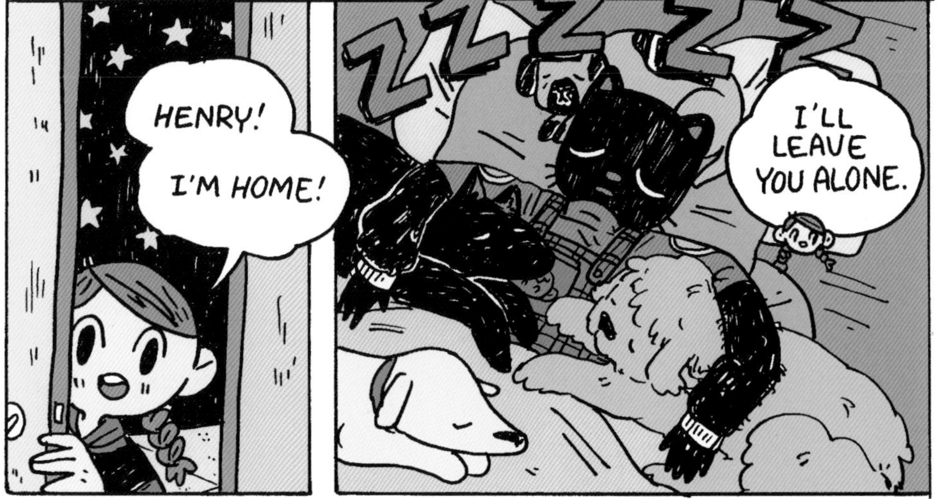
HENRY!
I'M HOME!
ZZZZZ
I'LL LEAVE YOU ALONE.

COOL
BOY.

HEY HENRY!
I GOT YOU SOMETHING.
WHAT DID YA GET?
A PRESENT!
"A PRESENT"?
YOU KNOW... A GIFT!
SOMETHING YOU'D GIVE TO A FRIEND OR A FAMILY MEMBER.
THIS IS YOURS NOW...
IT IS A VERY BEAUTIFUL BOX.
THANK YOU.

YOU'RE MISSING THE POINT!
OPEN IT!
OH, OKAY.
OOOOOOH!
AH!
I LOVE IT!
WORLD'S MOST CAT
OH! I'M SO GLAD! I--
COOL BOY
ITS SMALL. BUT I LIKE A CHALLENGE.
THAT'S NOT...
YOU KNOW ME SO WELL!
WORLD'S MOST CAT

SIGH
WORLD'S MOST CAT
HENRY

HMMM...

WHAT A THOUGHTFUL GIFT.

LICK LICK

TWEET
TWEE
I SHOULD DO SOMETHING NICE FOR HER.

THIS IS PERFECT.
OLIVE WILL LOVE THIS!

NOW I GOTTA MAKE IT PRETTY.

TOILET PAPER.

NICE!

A BOW!

I DID IT!

HENRY!
HELP ME WITH THE GROCERIES!
NO! I HAVE A BETTER IDEA!

WHAT'S GOING ON, HENRY?
TEEHEE

I GOT YOU A PRESENT!

OH, HENRY!
YOU SHOULDN'T HAVE!

DID YOU WRAP IT YOURSELF?
SO RESOURCEFUL --

AHHH!

DON'T YOU LIKE IT?
I-I LOVE IT...

COOL
"BOY"
COOL
BOY

HEY, OLIVE!?
WHAT?

I NEED YOUR HELP!

WHAT'S UP?

I HAVE TO FIND SOMETHING TO WEAR TO THIS PARTY!!
I CAN'T FIND ANYTHING TO WEAR!

DID YOU TAKE A SHOWER?
OF COURSE!
DUH!
LICK LICK
LICK LICK

OKAY...
LET ME HELP YOU FIND CLOTHES.
COOL

I WANNA LOOK COOL.
BUT, LIKE, REAL CHILL.

WOW.
YOU'RE REALLY STRESSING OVER THIS.
I WANNA IMPRESS MY FRIENDS!

AND WHO - ARE - THESE FRIENDS?

OH, YOU DON'T KNOW HER.
HER NAME IS MIMSY.
WANNA BE MY PLUS ONE?

CAN I?
OF COURSE!

MIMSY'S PARTIES ARE INCREDIBLE.
YOU'LL NEVER FORGET A MIMSY PARTY.

SHE'S ALWAYS GOT THE BEST FOOD...
...THE BEST GUESTS.

YOU'RE GONNA BE BLOWN AWAY.
WOW.
COOL BOY

YOU'RE MAKING ME NERVOUS!
AM I UNDERDRESSED?
YOU'RE FINE!

THIS PARTY SOUNDS LIKE A LOT.
I DON'T THINK I'M PREPARED.
SURE, IT'S THE HOTTEST PARTY IN TOWN.
BUT MIMSY'S SOOO COOL. YOU'LL LIKE HER.
COOL
COOL
MAYBE I SHOULD DO SOMETHING WITH MY HAIR REAL QUICK.
STOP WORRYING!
YOU'RE MAKING ME NERVOUS!

WOW! IS THIS IT?
NO, BUT WE'RE CLOSE!
ARE YOU SURE?

WE'RE HERE.
HUH?

HI, MIMSY!

THIS IS MY FRIEND OLIVE!

UM...
HI...
OH!
ARE THOSE HORS D'OEUVRES?

YOU SHOULD TRY THE RAT!
NO THANKS.

UM... HENRY...?
WHAT HAPPENED TO ALL THE TOILET PAPER?

I DON'T KNOW WHAT YOU'RE TALKING ABOUT!

HENRY.

FINE!
I ADMIT IT!

I NEVER USE YOUR PRECIOUS TOILET PAPER!
I PLAY WITH IT ONCE AND YOU FREAK OUT!
COOL
ARE YOU STILL USING THE LITTER BOX?
YEAH, SO WHAT!?

MAYBE IF YOU LEARNED TO USE THE TOILET...
... YOU'D LEARN TO APPRECIATE THE VALUE OF TOILET PAPER!
NOT GONNA HAPPEN!
I'LL NEVER LEARN!!
I GOTTA GO TO WORK!
I CAN'T DEAL WITH THIS RIGHT NOW.
THERE YOU GO AGAIN!
USING WORK TO AVOID CONFRONTATION.

STOP BEING STUPID!
WE'LL TALK ABOUT IT WHEN I GET HOME.

YEAH, SURE, WHATEVER.

IF OLIVE THINKS I'M JUST GONNA WAIT AROUND, SHE'S GOT ANOTHER THING COMING.

I CAN LIVE ON MY OWN.
PIZZA

I'LL HAVE MY OWN TOILET PAPER.
A KINGDOM OF TOILET PAPER...

AND I'LL INVITE EVERYONE!

EVERYONE BUT OLIVE!!

I GUESS ITS TIME FOR ME TO HIT THE ROAD.
THE WIDE OPEN ROAD.

THE TIME HAS COME FOR ME TO FORGE MY OWN PATH.
ALL ALONE.
ALL BY MY LONESOME.

MEOW
MEOW

MY NEW HOME!

I DON'T BELONG HERE.

HENRY!
I'M HOME!

HENRY?
WHERE ARE YOU?

HEN

SHAKE
HENRY

HI OLIVE.
HUFF
HUFF
HEY HENRY.

WE SHOULD ORDER SUSHI TONIGHT.
THAT SOUNDS NICE.

MY FAMILY IS GONNA LIKE YOU SO DON'T BE NERVOUS.
I'M NOT NERVOUS.

KNOCK
KNOCK

HELLO, OLIVE!
WHO'S YOUR FRIEND?

YOU'VE MET HENRY!
FORMER PET CAT, CURRENT ROOMMATE CAT.
NICE TO MEET YOU MRS. BRANCH.
YOU GOT TALLER.

SO, HOW'S ART SCHOOL?
I GRADUATED, LIKE, TWO YEARS AGO, MOM.
AND YOU'RE STILL WORKING AT THAT CAFE, HUH?
GO SAY HI TO YOUR DAD.
HE'S IN THE DEN.

HEY DAD.

OLIVE! HOW ARE YA?

I'M GOOD! I'M STILL WORKING AT THE CAFE--
YOU'D THINK WITH ALL THE MONEY WE SPENT ON ART SCHOOL YOU'D BE AN ARTIST BY NOW, HUH?

YEAH. YOU'D THINK...
HI, MR. BRANCH. I'M HENRY.

THIS SUCKS ALREADY.
I'M HAVING AN OKAY TIME.

OH, ITS MY BROTHER TWIG.

HEY TWIG.
WHATCHA DOIN'?

I'M PLAYING "SPACE GHOUL 2."
WANNA PLAY?

NO.
I DO!

PEOPLE SAY THE GRAPHICS ARE BETTER IN "SLIME TOWER."
BUT I THINK THE "SPACE GHOUL" SERIES HAS A MUCH BETTER STORY.

I'VE ONLY PLAYED ONE GAME BEFORE.
IT WAS CHECKERS AND I LOST.

DINNER'S READY!!
OKAY!

THIS IS NICE.

SO, HENRY.
WHAT DO YOU DO?
I DOGSIT.
IS THAT SOMETHING YOU HAVE TO GO TO SCHOOL FOR?

I DON'T KNOW WHAT SCHOOL IS.

AH, A SELF-MADE MAN!
IF ONLY OLIVE HAD YOUR LEVEL OF AMBITION.

I'VE HEARD ENOUGH.
I'M OUTTA HERE!

WAIT!
WOULD YOU LIKE TO TAKE SOME LEFTOVERS?
YES PLEASE!

SO HENRY, I'VE BEEN THINKING...
WE SHOULD GET A PET SINCE YOU'VE BECOME ALL INDEPENDENT AND HUMANISH.

WHAT'S THE POINT OF A PET?
I DON'T GET IT.

IT'S A COMPANION WHO YOU CARE FOR AND WHO LOVES YOU UNCONDITIONALLY!

I STILL DON'T GET IT.
LET'S GO TO THE PET SHOP.
YOU'LL MAKE THAT SPECIAL CONNECTION. YOU'LL SEE.
I THINK YOU'RE ANTHROPOMORPHISING THESE ANIMALS.

PET SHOP!

WOW!
HELLO CUTIES!

WE SHOULD HANG OUT IF YOU WANT.
THIS ISN'T WHAT I MEANT BY "SPECIAL CONNECTION."

WHAT ABOUT A DOG?

I DON'T THINK SO...
BARK
BARK
DEFINITELY NOT.

YOU BEING A CAT REALLY COMPLICATES THINGS.

RODENTS
Y'KNOW...
I'VE ALWAYS LIKED MICE.
THEY ARE PRETTY TASTY.
NOT TO EAT!

TWEET
YUM!

BON APPÉTIT!

MAYBE SOMETHING HERE WILL DO.
EXOTIC PETS

ARE THESE STILL PETS?

OLIVE!

I THINK I'VE MADE A "SPECIAL CONNECTION."

REALLY!?

LOOK AT IT.

IT'S LIKE HE'S STARING RIGHT INTO MY SOUL.
...REALLY?
CAN WE TAKE IT HOME?

SURE.
I'M NAMING HIM RUPERT.

WELCOME TO YOUR NEW HOME RUPERT.

OH!
HE'S EATING HIS LETTUCE!

HE'S AMAZING.

IT'S PRETTY CUTE...
... I GUESS.

GROAN
WHAT WAS THAT?

GROAN
OLIVE!

WHY AREN'T YOU READY FOR WORK?

I'M SICK! I CAN'T GO TO WORK TODAY!

YOU LOOK TERRIBLE.
I KNOW.
ARE YOU...
...DYING?
NO!

SO WHAT DO YOU DO WHEN YOU'RE SICK?

EAT SOUP, DRINK TEA, SLEEP.

I'LL HELP!

DON'T YOU WORRY ABOUT A THING!
JUST KEEP RELAXING AND BEING SWEATY.

TEA... TEA... TEA...
HOW DOES OLIVE USUALLY MAKE TEA?

HOT WATER!

GOT 'EM!

HERE YOU GO!
BE CAREFUL. IT IS VERY HOT TEA!

IS THIS JUST HOT WATER AND LEAVES?
YEAH, TEA!!

SOUP...
SOUP...
SOUP...

SOUP!

I CAN'T EAT THIS !

WHY NOT !?

IT'S A SLICE OF PIZZA IN HOT WATER.
YOU CAN PUT ANYTHING IN A SOUP!

HEY, OLIVE?
KNOCK
KNOCK

OLIVE?

ARE YOU DEAD?

I DON'T THINK DEAD BODIES SNORE...

I'M SURE SHE WON'T MIND IF I TAKE A NAP HERE.

HEY, OLIVE?
I HAVE A QUESTION!
YEAH?

WHY DON'T WE HAVE ANY FURNITURE?

IT'S WEIRD.
I'VE NEVER NEEDED IT.
IT'S NOT LIKE I HAVE PEOPLE OVER.

PLUS, I'M A MINIMALIST.

NO YOU'RE NOT!
I'VE SEEN YOUR CLOSET!

HONESTLY, I JUST NEVER HAVE THE MONEY.

I HAVE THE MONEY!

WHAT?
HOW?

DOGSITTING!
I MAKE RENT WITH TWO DAYS OF WORK AND I DUNNO WHAT TO DO WITH THE REST.

SEE?
SO THAT'S WHY MY MATTRESS FEELS SO LUMPY!
FANCY CAT

I CAN'T BELIEVE MY CAT MAKES MORE MONEY THAN ME.

I REALLY DON'T FEEL COMFORTABLE LUGGING ALL OF THIS CASH AROUND.
IT'S FINE! NOBODY KNOWS!

IS THIS REALLY ALL JUST FROM DOGSITTING.

THIS IS JUST TIPS!
MY BIG MONEY IS IN A VERY SECRET PLACE.

HOW!?

I'M SUPER GOOD AT MY JOB!

FURNITURE PARTY
I'VE NEVER BEEN IN A FURNITURE STORE BEFORE!
LOOK AT ALL THESE COUCHES!
THIS IS NICE!
STOP THAT!

SCRATCH
SCRATCH
SALE!
THIS IS NICE TOO!
PLEASE STOP DOING THAT!!
EXCUSE ME, SIR.
YOU BREAK, YOU BUY!
MANAGER
OOPS!
THIS IS NICE!

HEY, OLIVE!
WHAT'S A BIRTHDAY PARTY?

IT'S A PARTY TO CELEBRATE THE DAY YOU WERE BORN.

WHEN WAS I BORN?

I DUNNO, YOU WERE A STRAY.
THE VET SAYS YOU'RE PROBABLY AROUND THREE YEARS OLD.

I DON'T HAVE A BIRTHDAY...
LET'S JUST PICK A DAY!

I WANT MY BIRTHDAY TO BE TODAY!

THAT'S TOO SHORT NOTICE!
I'M NOT PREPARED!

GET PREPARED!

WHAT ARE YOU DOING?
TEXTING EVERYONE.

OKAY!
I'VE GOTTA GO GET SOME STUFF.
·CAKE
PARTY HATS
·BALLOONS

I'LL BE RIGHT BACK.

PARTY ZONE!
PLATES
CAKE
SALE
HATS

3ISH

I'M BACK!

OLIVE!

UH...
I BROUGHT HATS.

WE'RE LIKE PARTY WIZARDS!
ARE THESE ALL YOUR PRESENTS?
YEP!

LET'S GO MINGLE!
KEEP OUT!
GET OUTTA MY ROOM!
COOL
HAPPY B
WAKE UP, OLIVE!
CAN I HAVE ANOTHER BIRTHDAY TONIGHT?

COOL
BØY
HEY!

OLIVE!
I'M BORED!
I'M BUSY!!
BUT I'M BORED!!
I GOTTA GO TO MY LIFE DRAWING CLASS.
CAN I COME!?
... OKAY.
THANK YOU!!

I'M GLAD WE'RE DOING THIS!!
YOU ALWAYS SAY I NEED TO FIND A HOBBY.
COOL BOY

WELL, THERE'S A LOT YOU SHOULD KNOW.
TELL ME!

ART TAKES A LOT OF PRACTICE!
AND LOTS OF DISCIPLINE.

AND IT'S NOT ENOUGH TO JUST BE GOOD.
YOU HAVE TO MAKE SOMETHING INTERESTING.
FASCINATING.

DON'T BE DISCOURAGED IF YOU DON'T GET IT RIGHT AWAY!
ART PARTY!
I'VE BEEN AT IT FOR YEARS AND I'M STILL WORKING AT IT.
I'LL WORK MY HARDEST!
YOU'LL DO FINE!
SAD
ART PARTY!
IT'S SAD IN HERE!

OH MY GOODNESS!

SHE'S NAKED!
LIKE SOME KIND OF HOUSE CAT!

THAT'S HOW WE LEARN THE HUMAN FORM!

WHAT DO I DO WITH THIS?
PUT IT ON THE PAPER AND MOVE IT AROUND TO MAKE MARKS.

YOU GOTTA DRAW THAT NAKED LADY!!
WOW!!

IT MIGHT BE TOUGH FOR A WHILE
BUT IT GETS EASIER!
THIS IS FUN!

IN THE END, IT DOESN'T MATTER IF YOU'RE GOOD OR NOT AS LONG AS YOU'RE HAVING A GOOD TIME.

AMAZING!
WOW!!

LOOK, OLIVE!
MY FIRST DRAWING!
WHAT DO YOU THINK?

IT'S GOOD.
SNAP

COOL BOY
COOL BOY
COOL BOY
COOL BOY
COOL BOY
COOL BOY
COOL BOY

OLIVE!
WHAT ARE YOU DOING!?
HONING MY CRAFT.
STOP IT!

WHAT? WHY?
BECAUSE...

... TONIGHT IS OUR SLUMBER PARTY!

GO PUT ON YOUR CUTEST PAJAMAS.
QUICKLY BEFORE OUR GUESTS ARRIVE!

I DON'T REMEMBER AGREEING TO THIS!!
IT'S A SURPRISE PARTY!
SURPRISE!

DING DONG
THEY'RE HERE!
HI EVERYBODY!
THAT WAS FAST.
OLIVE, YOU KNOW DIXIE!
HI!
AND THIS IS FRAN.
I DOGSIT FOR HER.
MY DACHSHUND'S NAME IS QUARK.
AND THAT'S SCRAPPY!
MROW.
I NAMED MY DOG QUARK AFTER THE DOG FROM "HONEY, I SHRUNK THE KIDS."
OK.

I'M HAPPY YOU COULD ALL MAKE IT TO MY FIRST SLUMBER PARTY!

SO WHAT NOW, HENRY?

LET'S PLAY TRUTH OR DARE!
DARE ME TO EAT A WORM!?
I'LL DO IT!!

WHO WOULD MAKE YOU DO SUCH A CRUEL THING?

I'VE GOT A BETTER IDEA!

I HEARD THAT SLUMBER PARTIES ARE A GOOD PLACE TO TALK ABOUT BOYS YOU LIKE...

CAN I START!?
YES!

I'D LIKE TO TALK ABOUT MY DACHSHUND PUPPY.
QUARK IS NICE.
HE LIKES TO SLEEP ON MY PILLOW.
I LIKE HIM A LOT.
1984

WONDERFUL!

THE BOY I LIKE MOST... HMM...
I LIKE OLD MAN BILLY BECAUSE HE FEEDS THE BIRDS EVERY DAY SO I ALWAYS GET A MIDDAY SNACK.

WHAT ABOUT YOU, SCRAPPY?
MOW.
HOW SCANDALOUS!

I DON'T LIKE BOYS.
I DON'T THINK WE'RE DOING THIS RIGHT.
SHOULD WE ORDER PIZZA NOW?
YES!
MOW.
I ALWAYS KEEP A COPY OF MY FAVORITE MOVIE WITH ME!

Cool
Boy

I DON'T THINK I'M DRESSED FOR HIKING.

BUT YA LOOK GOOD!

I DON'T THINK NATURE CARES ABOUT MY FRESHLY SHAVED LEGS.

THAT'S WHY I DON'T SHAVE.

YOU DON'T SHAVE 'CUS YOU'RE A CAT!
EXACTLY!

CAN WE TAKE A BREAK?
BUT WE'RE SO CLOSE TO THE CAMPSITE.

I THINK I'M DYING.

DRINK SOME WATER!!

HENRY

LICK LICK
HENRY

YOU WANT SOME?
HENRY
NO THANKS.

SUIT YOURSELF!
LICK
LICK
HENRY

WE'RE HERE!
FINALLY.
IT'S EMPTY!
YEAH, WE HAVE TO PITCH OUR TENT!
I THOUGHT CAMP SITES CAME WITH TENTS!
THEY DON'T!

HERE, I BORROWED A TENT FROM MY AUNT.

LET'S DO IT!!
Cool

THIS ISN'T RIGHT.

I THINK IT LOOKS GREAT!
Cool

I'M STARVING.
LET'S START A FIRE!

HA!
HOW'S A FIRE GONNA SATIATE YOUR HUNGER?
WE USE THE FIRE TO COOK!
WHAT!? NO! YOU JUST CLICK BUTTONS ON THE MICROWAVE!
Cool
Boy

YOU GOT SOME CRAZY IDEAS, OLIVE!
HA HA!

WOW!
IT'S SO PRETTY!
WHAT ARE YOU DOING!?
COOKING MARSHMALLOWS OVER THE FIRE!
I WANNA TRY.
WHERE'D YOU GET THAT BIRD?
IN THE WOODS!
THIS IS FANTASTIC!
CAN WE STAY HERE FOREVER?
Cool
NO WAY!
YOU'RE NOT AN OUTDOOR CAT.

AAACK!!
WHAT THE...?

COUGH!!
COUGH!!
HENRY?

OLIVE!
I THINK I'M DYING!!

YOU'RE PROBABLY JUST SICK.
I KNOW! I'M HAVING A PROBLEM!

AND THAT PROBLEM IS DEATH!!

YOU'RE NOT DYING!! YOU'RE JUST SICK! LET'S TAKE YOU TO THE VET.

VET CLINIC

HENRY?

I'M SCARED.
I'LL HOLD YOUR HAND

YOU'VE GOTTEN BIGGER SINCE THE LAST TIME I SAW YOU.

YES.
THANK YOU.

SO WHAT'S THE PROBLEM?
HE'S HAD A TERRIBLE COUGH ALL MORNING.

ALRIGHT, WELL, LETS SEE WHAT—
COUGH!

IT'S A GIANT HAIRBALL.

SO WHAT NOW?

YOU HAVE TO START USING THE SHOWER.

WHAT!?
WHY?

BECAUSE LICKING YOURSELF CLEAN LED TO THIS!

BUT OLIVE!
YOU KNOW HOW I FEEL ABOUT WATER!

I WON'T DO IT!

GASP!!
PSSSS

PSSS

PSSSS

LICK LICK
PSSSSS
LICK

HEY HENRY! HOW WAS YOUR FIRST SHOWER?

UM... RELAXING?
GOOD!

HACK
COUGH

COOL
BOY

OLIVE!!
SOMETHING WEIRD IS HAPPENING!
WHAT'S WRONG!?
MY BODY IS CHANGING!
AND I HATE CHANGE!
LOOK!
SO SOFT!
WHAT IS HAPPENING TO MY BODY!?
YOU'RE JUST GAINING A LIL BIT OF WEIGHT.
IT'S PROBABLY ALL THE PIZZA.

IF YOU'RE WORRIED ABOUT IT, THERE ARE THINGS WE CAN DO ABOUT IT!

TELL ME!
TELL ME!

WE CAN DIET AND EXERCISE!

GOSH, OLIVE!
YOU'RE SO, SO SMART!
PET
PET
THANKS.

SO WHAT DO WE DO NOW?

PUT ON SOME WORKOUT CLOTHES!

COOL!
NICE!
YEAH!
GREAT!

NOW LET'S GO FOR A RUN?!

YEAH!

IT'S RAINING.

LET'S DO THIS SOME OTHER TIME.
YEAH!

LET'S TRY TO WORKOUT RIGHT HERE.

GENIUS.

PUSHUPS!

OK!

PLOP!!

PHEW!
THAT WAS A HARD PUSH UP!

WE DIDN'T EVEN GET TO THE "UP" PART!

WELL, I THINK WE SHOULD TREAT OURSELVES!

HOW?

HELLO? PIZZAZONE?
YES, IT'S ME HENRY.

HENRY!
PIZZA IS THE ENEMY!

DON'T WORRY!
I GOT THIS!

I'D LIKE TWO LARGE DIET PIZZAS!
...OH, I SEE...
THEN JUST GIMME THE USUAL.
SIGH

HEY, OLIVE!
THE INTERNET TAUGHT ME ABOUT "OBSCENE GESTURES" AND —.
I DON'T HAVE TIME FOR THIS!
O K
WHAT'S GOING ON WITH YOU TODAY?
I'VE GOT A JOB INTERVIEW TODAY!
BUT YOU ALREADY HAVE A JOB!
I NEED A BETTER ONE!
CAN I COME?
OK, BUT YOU HAVE TO BE GOOD.!!

SO WHAT'S THIS JOB YOU'RE TRYING TO GET?
IT'S JUST SOME GRAPHIC DESIGN JOB FOR SOME SOUP COMPANY.
IT'D BE NICE TO WORK IN THE ARTS.

I'M A LITTLE SCARED THAT I MIGHT BE UNDER QUALIFIED FOR THIS JOB.

THE WORST CASE SCENARIO IS YOU DON'T GET THE JOB AND YOU KEEP ON TRYING!

AND MAYBE YOU KEEP FAILING FOREVER AND HAVE TO KEEP WORKING AT THE COFFEE SHOP UNTIL YOU DIE!

OK.
HERE WE GO.

YOU CAN DO IT.

HI, I'M HERE FOR AN INTERVIEW.
I'M HERE FOR FUN.
ALRIGHT!
FOLLOW ME.

THE BOSS WILL SEE YOU NOW.
THANK YOU.

CAN I COME?
NO!
BUT I'M BORED!

HELLO, I'M OLIVE.
I'M HENRY.
I'M HERE FOR FUN.
DO IT
OK...
SO I SEE YOU WORKED FOR THE BEAN ZONE COFFEE SHOP.
YES SIR.
BUT YOUR PORTFOLIO DOESN'T SEEM TO EXHIBIT ANY OF THE WORK YOU DID FOR THE COMPANY.
WELL, ACTUALLY...
I WAS JUST A BARISTA...
OH...
I SEE.

WELL, I'M GOING TO BE FRANK HERE, MS. BRANCH.
I DON'T THINK YOU'RE QUALIFIED TO WORK AT OUR SOUP COMPANY.
YOU LACK EXPERIENCE.

BUT YOU LIKED MY PORTFOLIO...
PLEASE LEAVE.

OK.

OH, WAIT?! MR. BOSS?
YES?

OK

HEY, HENRY?
YES?
I THINK IT'S TIME TO GO GROCERY SHOPPING.
I HAVE AN IDEA!
OH, NO...
NO, IT'S A GOOD THING!!
YOU'VE BEEN WORKING SO HARD TRYING TO FIND A NEW JOB!
SO LET ME GO SHOPPING FOR YOU!
I DUNNO, HENRY...
I'LL DO A VERY GOOD JOB.

OK, WELL... TAKE THIS LIST.
I'LL GUARD IT WITH MY LIFE.
GOOD LUCK.
TOILET PAPER!
DON'T FORGET!
BYE BYE!
DOG PARK
WHOOSH
NO!
LIST
· TOILET PAP
· MILK
· EGGS
· cheese
· bread
· honey
· rice
· tea
· cereal

SNIFF
SNIFF

CHOMP

NOOOO!!
BAD DOG!
BAD DOG!

SIR!
CONTROL YOUR HELL HOUND!
WHATEVER.

WHAT AM I GONNA DO?
OLIVE WILL NEVER TRUST ME AGAIN!!

I'LL HAVE TO IMPROVISE!!!

SHOP MART

ALRIGHT!

OLIVE DOES
LIKE THESE...
SALE
TAMPONS
TAMPONS
TAMPONS

HERE YA
GO!!
SALE

I'M HOME!
OLIVE!
HOW DID IT GO?
I THINK IT WENT WELL!
TAMPONS
TUNA
SARDINES
CHOCO
HENRY.
WHAT HAPPENED TO THE LIST I GAVE YOU?
IT GOT EATEN.
OH SHOOT! I FORGOT TO GET THE TOILET PAPER.

WHAT THE HECK!?

WHAT'S HAPPENING?

I GOT A WEIRD TEXT FROM JEAN.

LEMME SEE!

HI, OLIVE.
I KNOW IT'S A BIT RANDOM BUT I WAS WONDERING IF YOU WOULD JOIN ME FOR LUNCH TODAY?

HE'S IN LOVE WITH YOU!

NO HE'S NOT. BUT ITS WEIRD RIGHT?

WHAT IF IT'S A PRANK?

IT'S NOT A PRANK!
IT'S ROMANCE!

I DON'T EVEN THINK I LIKE BOYS.

BUT HE IS CUTE AND SOFT.

COOL BOY
YOU KNOW...
I DID THINK HE WAS CUTE WHEN WE FIRST MET...
BUT I HAVEN'T BEEN ON A DATE IN YEARS.

WEAR THIS.

O K
IT'S JUST A LAST MINUTE LUNCH DATE.
IT'S PROBABLY JUST, LIKE, A FRIEND DATE.

NONSENSE.

NOW, LET ME GIVE YOU SOME ADVICE FROM WHAT I'VE LEARNED AS A SUAVE CAT.

IF HE SHOWS INTEREST, START MEOWING. HARD. ALMOST LIKE A HOWL.
THEN LET HIM SNIFF YOUR RUMP AND ——
NO.

THAT'S NOT WHAT HUMAN PEOPLE DO.

I'M READY.

BEAUTIFUL!

I FEEL LIKE I'M GONNA DIE.

THERE HE IS

HI JEAN.
OLIVE! HEY!

I KNOW IT SEEMS ODD FOR ME TO ASK YOU TO LUNCH LIKE THIS.
BUT I HAVE TO ASK YOU SOMETHING.
yes?
A PAL OF MINE IS STARTING AN ARTIST WORKSHOP FOR KIDS AND YOU'RE THE ONLY ARTIST I REALLY KNOW.
SO I WAS WONDERING IF YOU'RE INTERESTED IN TEACHING KIDS.
OH... YEAH, SURE...
HENRY!?
HOW WAS IT?
IT WASN'T A DATE! IT WAS A JOB OFFER!
I'M SO SORRY.
PET PET

I don't

WHO IS BENJI NATE?

BENJI WAS BORN IN PUERTO RICO IN 1994; EXACTLY EIGHT MONTHS AFTER THE FIRST CHUPACABRA SIGHTING ON THE ANNIVERSARY OF THE ROSWELL UFO INCIDENT.

COINCIDENCE? PROBABLY NOT.

Best

Friends